Year End Closing Activities

S/4 HANA

SAP S/4HANA Year End Closing

Year End Activities

Once the Periodic closer activities are perform the business must and Execute year End closing activities in Financial Account to carry forward Financial accounting Transaction to one fiscal year to Next to fiscal year

Pre-Requirement :

1. Check Retained Earning account

Retained Earnings Account is used to carry forward the balance from one fiscal year to the next fiscal year. You can assign a Retained Earning Account to each P&L account in the chart of accounts (COA).

2. Create Gender ledger Account for Retained Earning Accounts

Provide search text as "MANAGE G/L ACCOUNT MASTER DATA" and click enter

And click on Manage G/L Account Master Data

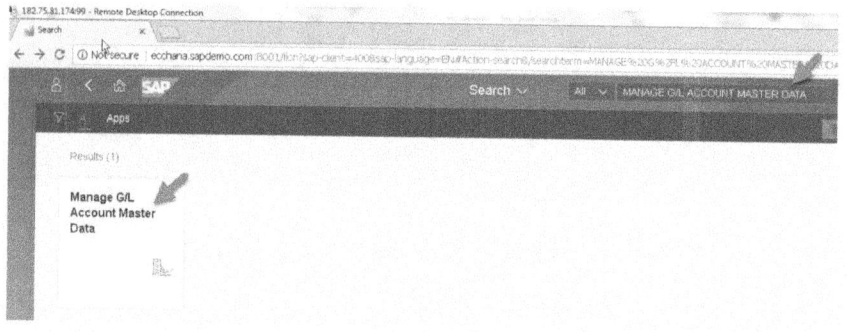

Click on '+' symbol

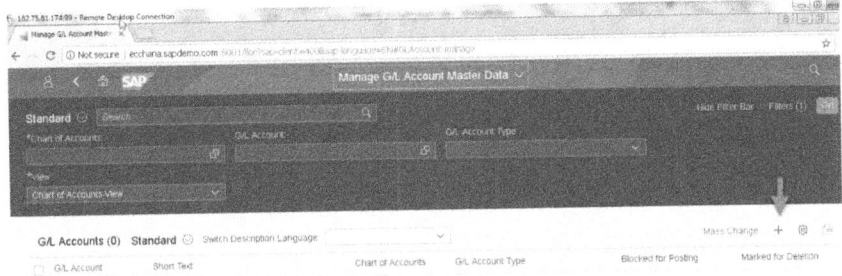

Provide new G/L account number

Chart of accounts as "YCOA"

Provide short text and long text

Select account type as "Gender Account (General)" and Account group as "SAKO"

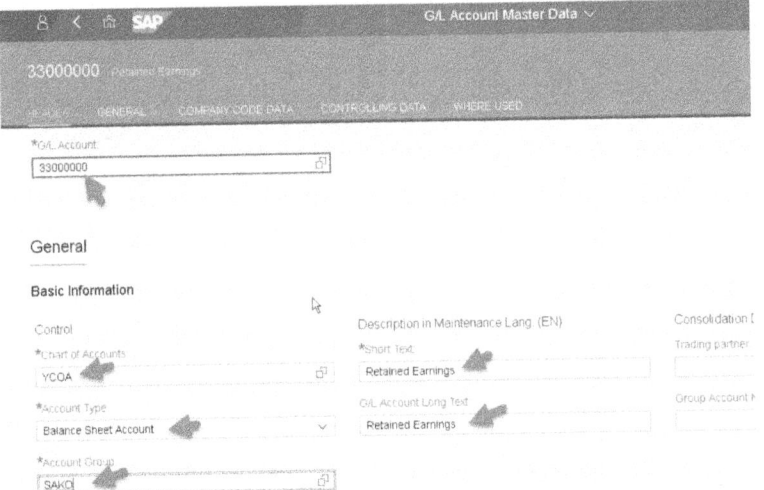

Click Company Code Data

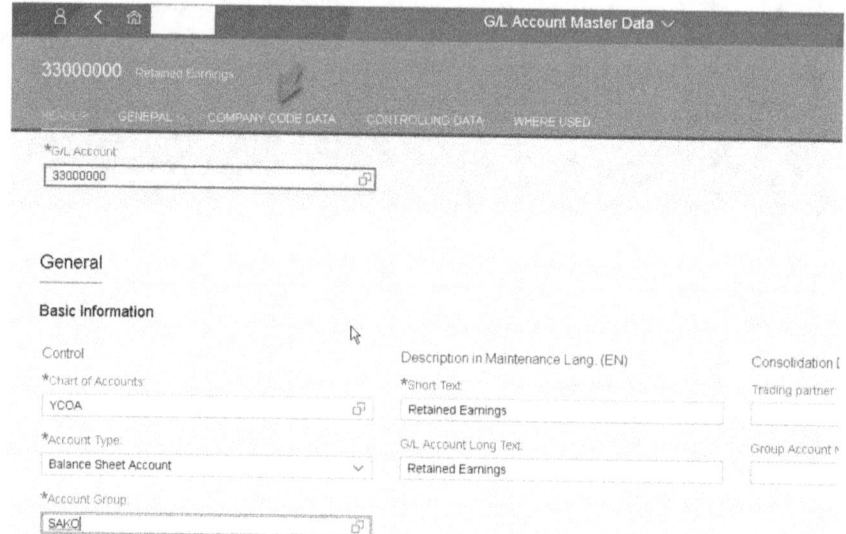

Click '+' symbol

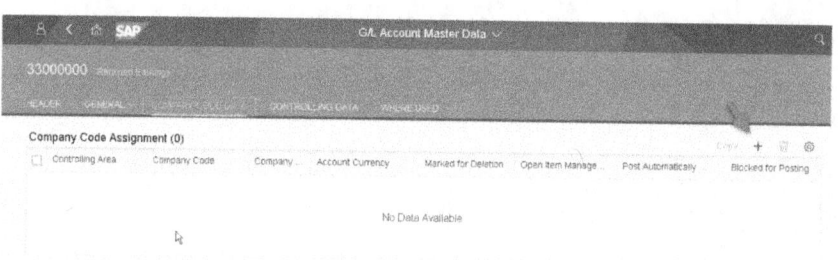

Provide New Company code assignment as "1010"

Account currency as "EUR"

Select the check box for Only balance in Local Currency

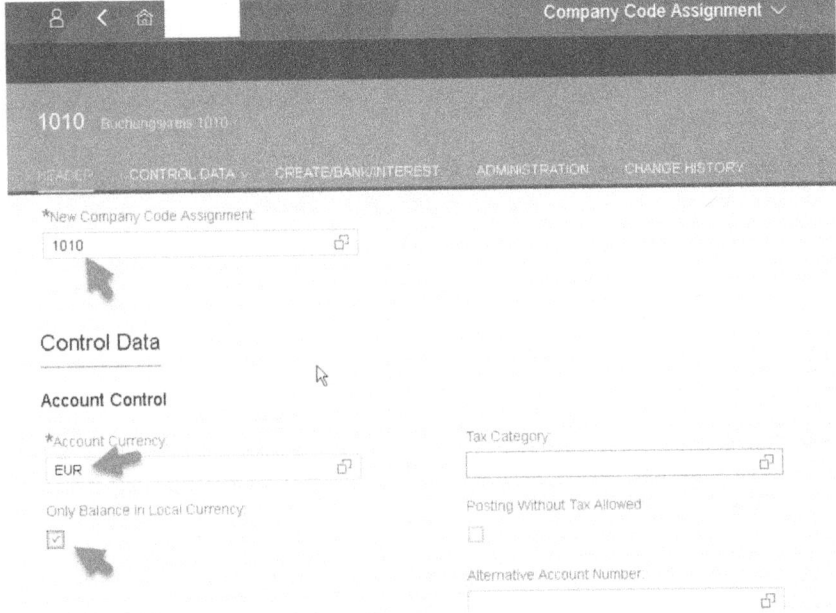

Provide the Sort key for "01"

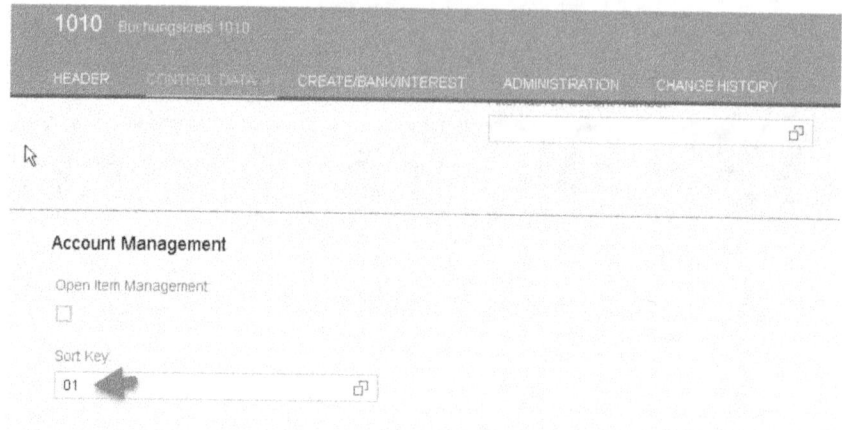

Provide Field Status Group as "YB01"

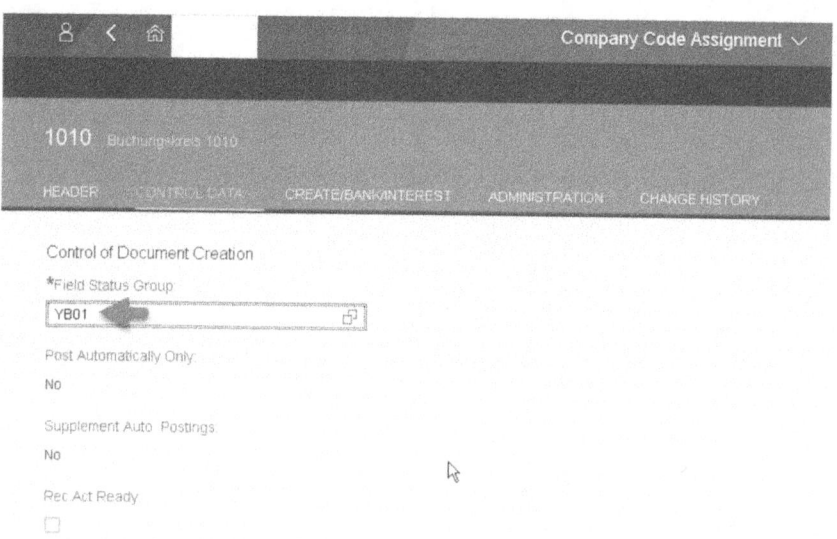

Click ok

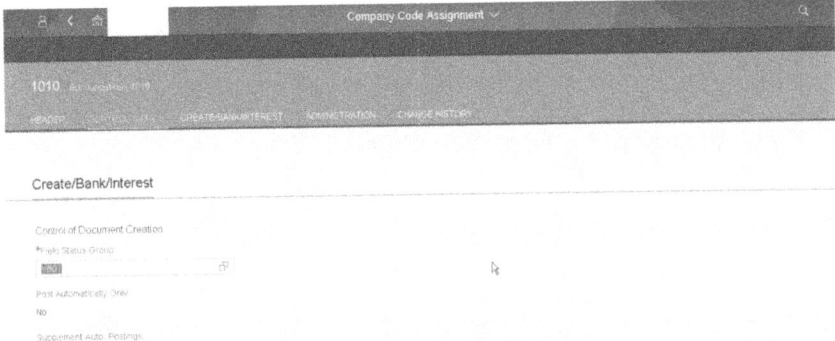

Click Controlling Data

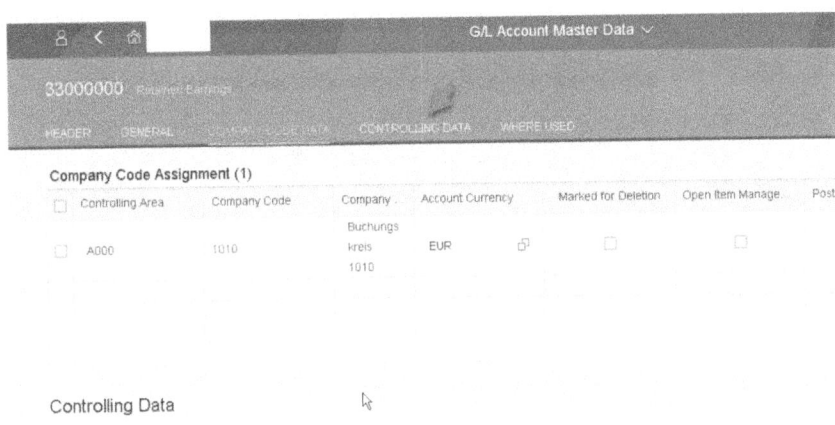

Controlling Data

Click on save

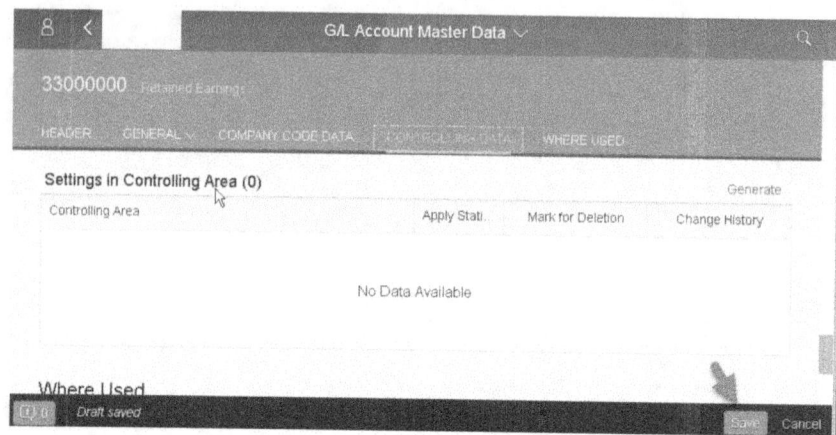

Here we see data was saved

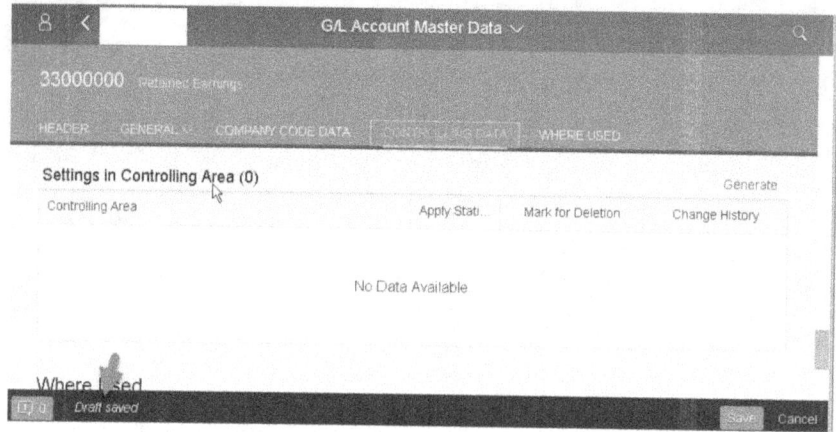

G/L Account Master Data

10011100 ASSET

HEADER | GENERAL | COMPANY CODE DATA | CONTROLLING DATA | WHERE USED

*G/L Account:
10011100

General

Basic Information

Control

*Chart of Accounts:
9000

*Account Type:
Primary Costs or Revenue

*Account Group:
1000

Description in Maintenance Lang. (EN)

*Short Text:
ASSET

G/L Account Long Text:
BANK ASSET

Consolid...

Trading pa...

Group Acc...

Draft saved

3. Define Retained Earnings Account

SPRO→ Financial Accounting(New) → Gender Ledger Accounting(New) → Master Data → G/l Account → Preparations → Define Retained Earnings Account

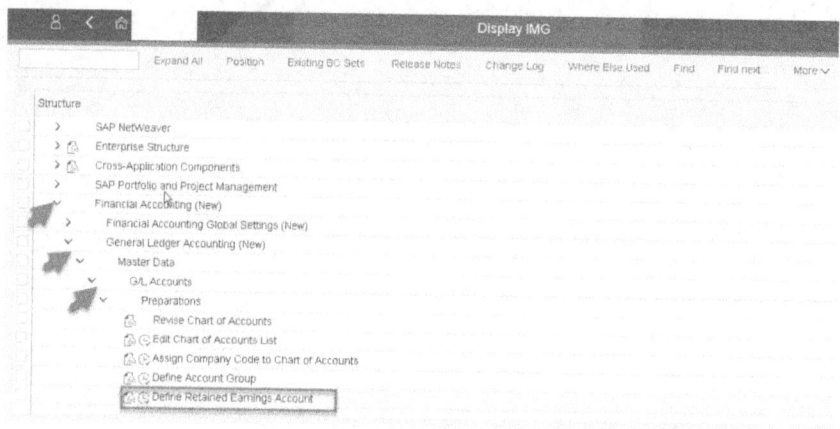

Enter the Chart of Accounts

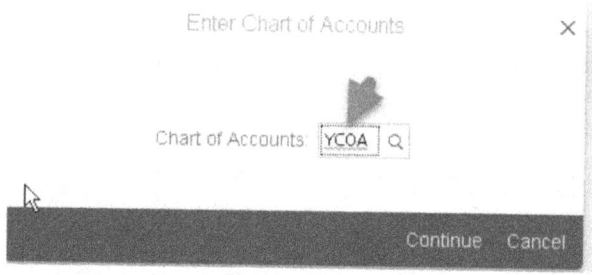

Click on Continue button

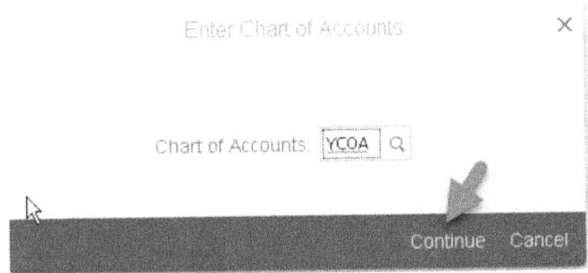

Here we see No Retrained Earning Account is not assign

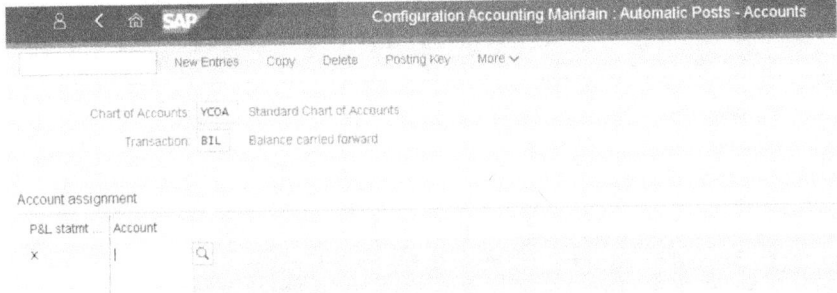

Enter the Retrained Earning A/c

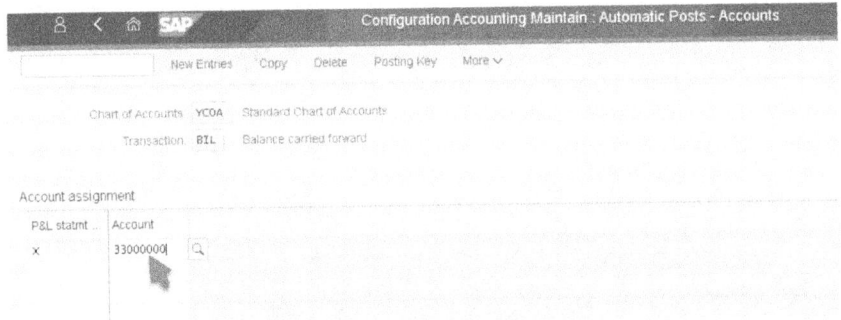

Click on Save button

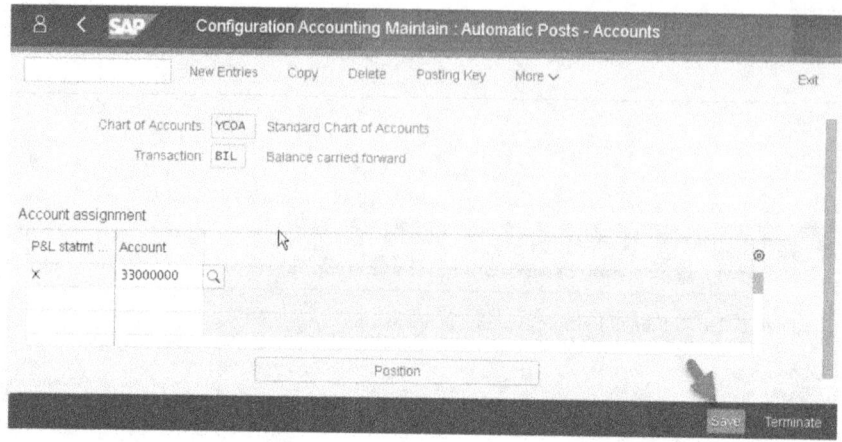

Click on continue

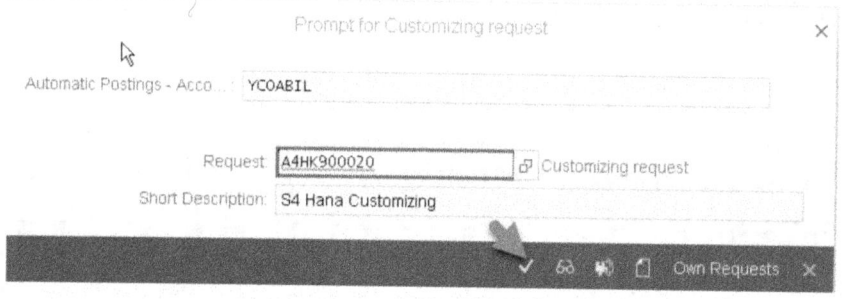

Here we see changes have been made

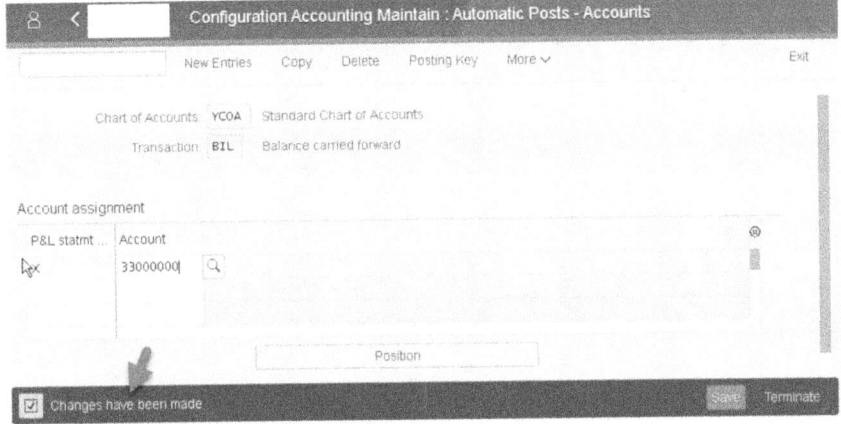

4. Copy Document Number Ranges to New Fiscal Year

SPRO → Financial Accounting (New) → Financial Accounting Global Ledger (New) → Document → Document Number Ranges → Document Entry View → Copy to Fiscal year (OBH2)

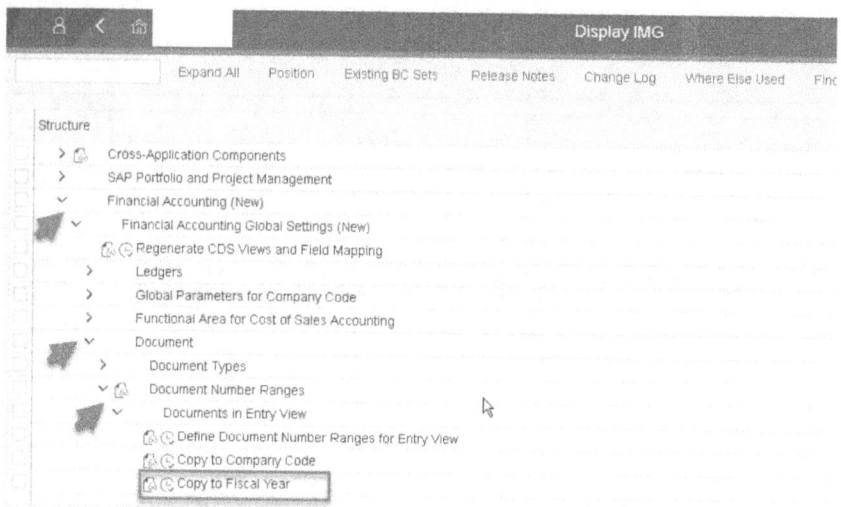

Click to Enter for the Number Ranges

Transport Number Range Intervals

The number range intervals are not included in automatic recording of customizing changes. Transport of all the changes made within number range interval maintenance must be triggered manually.

In the initial screen for number range interval maintenance choose the function Interval -> Transport.

Please note the information that you get when transporting number range intervals.

Enter the Company code, From & To Number Range

Document Number Ranges: Copy to Fiscal Year

General selections
- Company code: 1010   to:
- Number range number: 01   to: ZZ

Source fiscal year details
- *To fiscal year:

Target fiscal year details
- *To fiscal year:

Enter Current Fiscal year

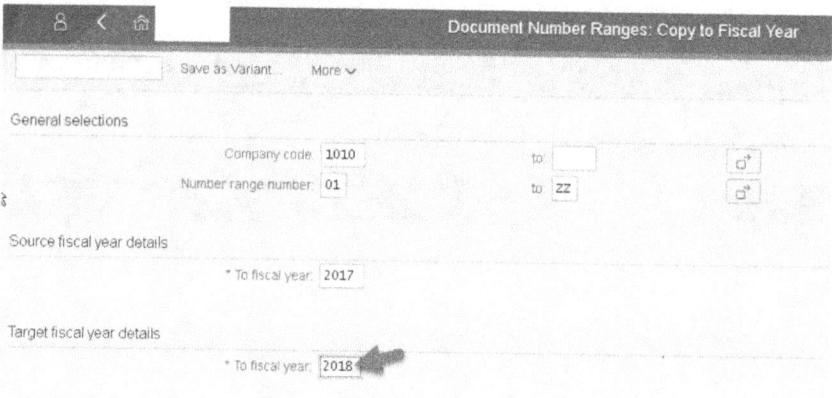

Enter the To Fiscal Year

Click on Execute

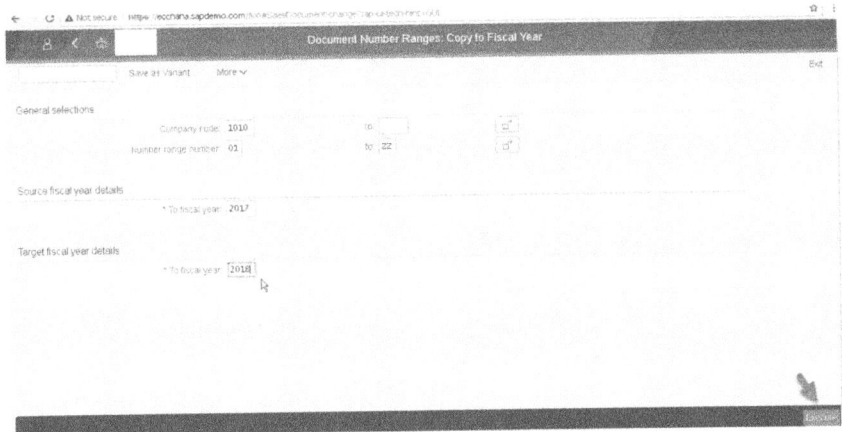

Select to Yes button to confirm

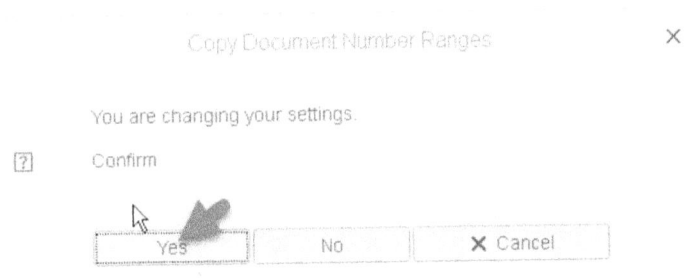

Here we see All Number Ranges copy from one Fiscal to New Fiscal year

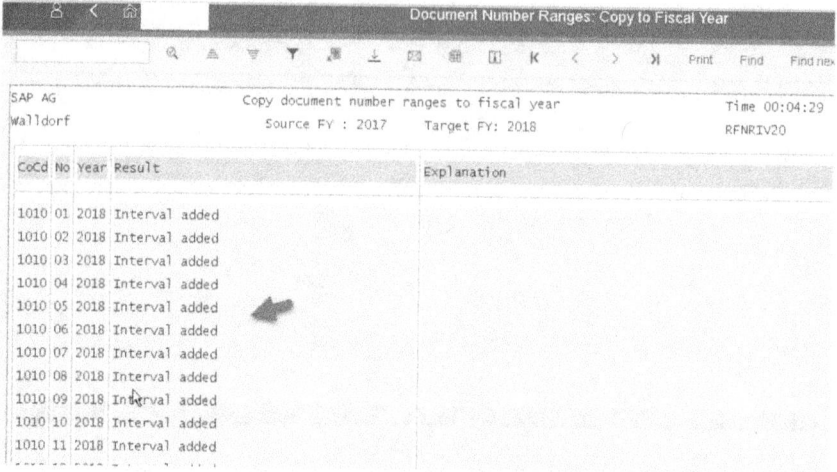

5. Checking for Number Ranges for New Fiscal year

SPRO → Financial Accounting (New) → Financial Accounting Global settings (New) → Document → Document Number Ranges → Document Entry View → Define Document Number Ranges for Entry View (FBN1)

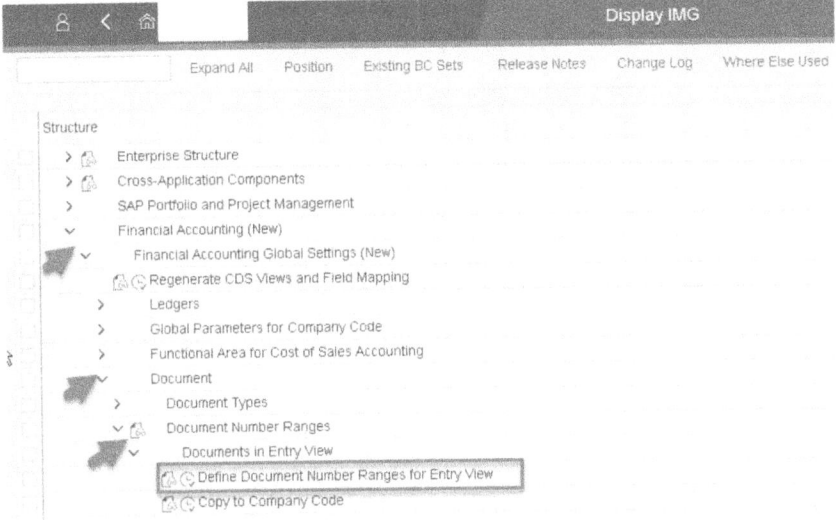

Enter the Company code

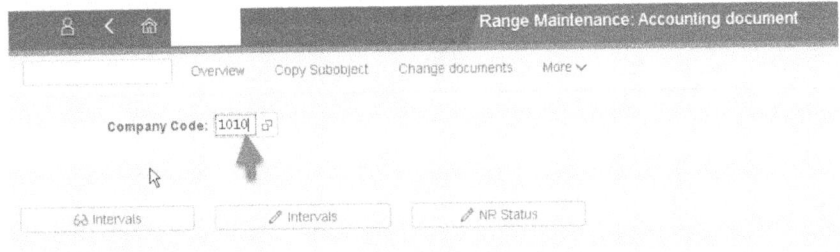

Click on Change Intervals button

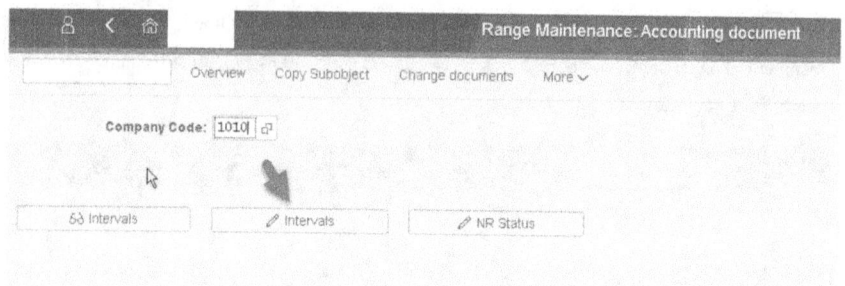

Here we see All Number Updated on New fiscal year for 2018

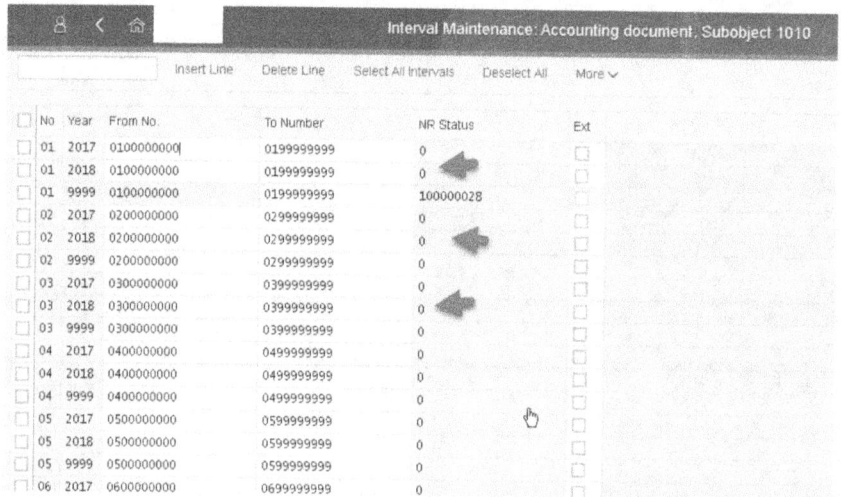

6. Carry forward Account Receivable and Accounts Payable

Accounting → Financial Accounting → Accounts Receivable → Periodic Processing → Closing → Carry Forward → Balance Carry Forward (F-07)

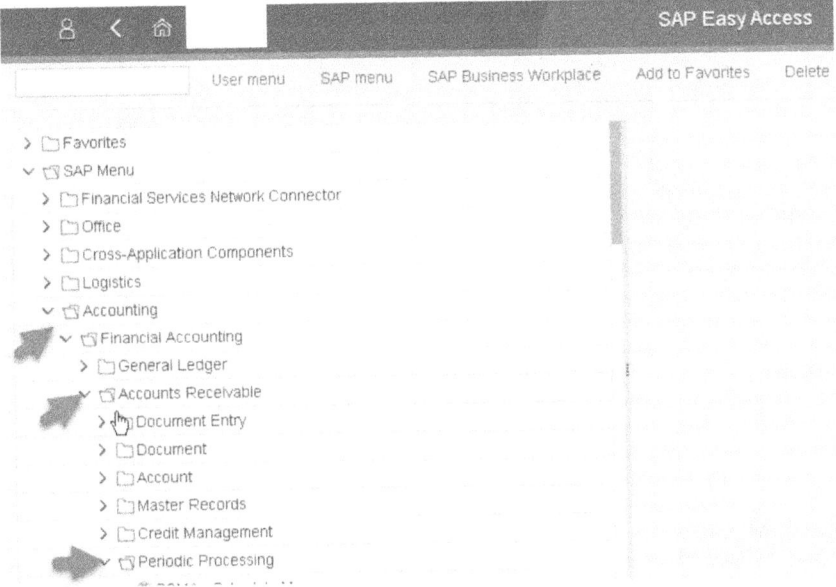

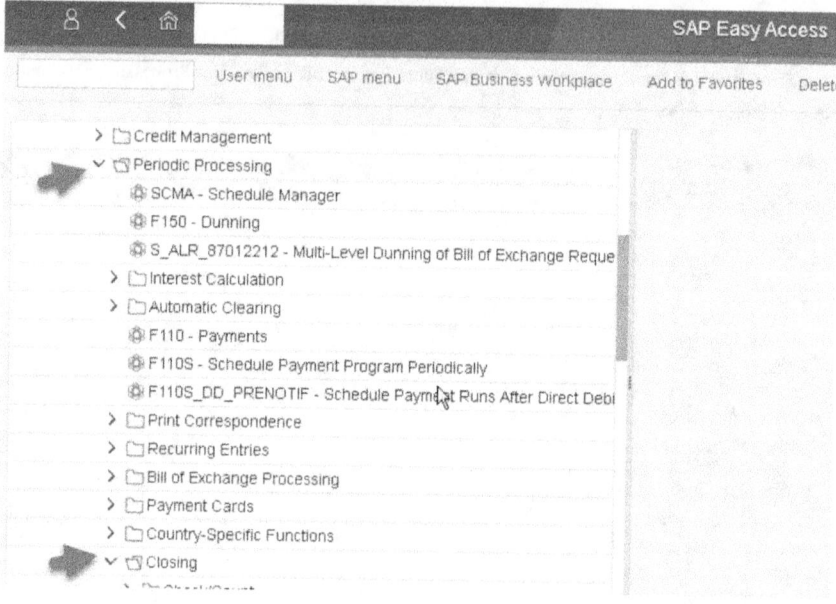

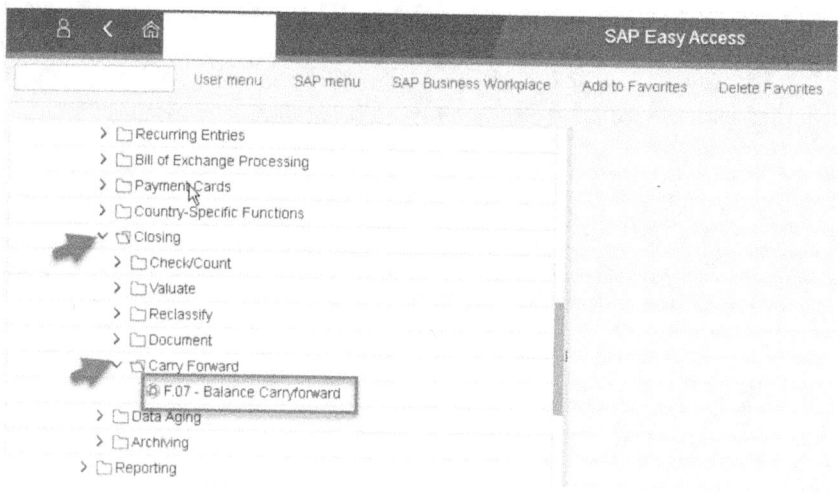

Enter the company code

Enter the carry forward fiscal year

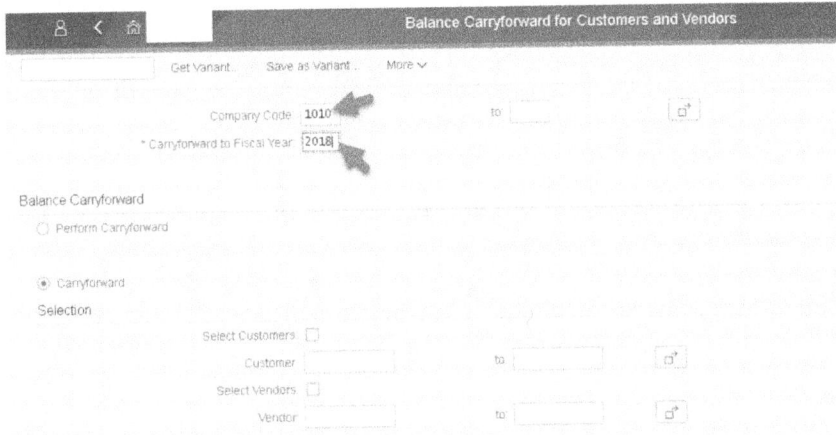

Select check box for Carry forward

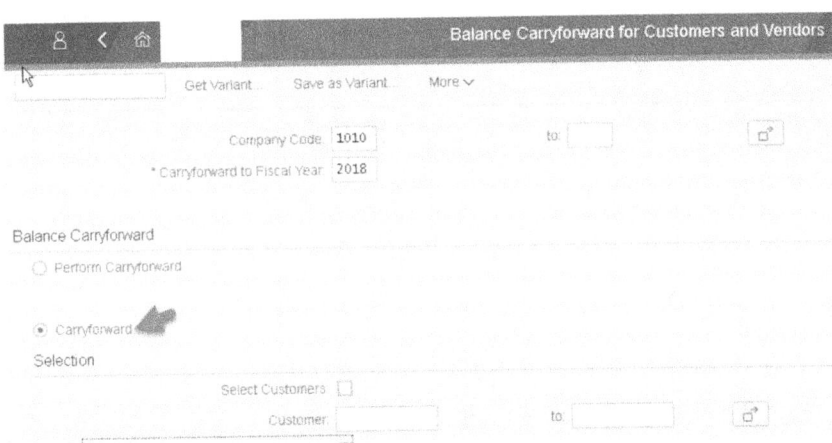

Select the check box for customer and Vendor

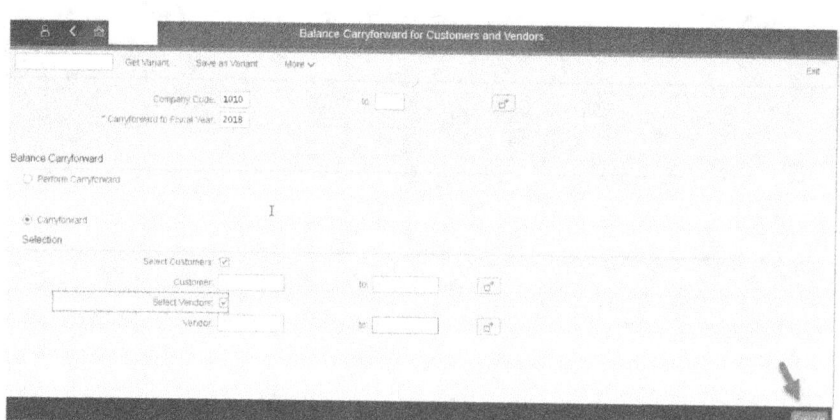

Click to Execute button

Here we see Balance is Success fully carry forward

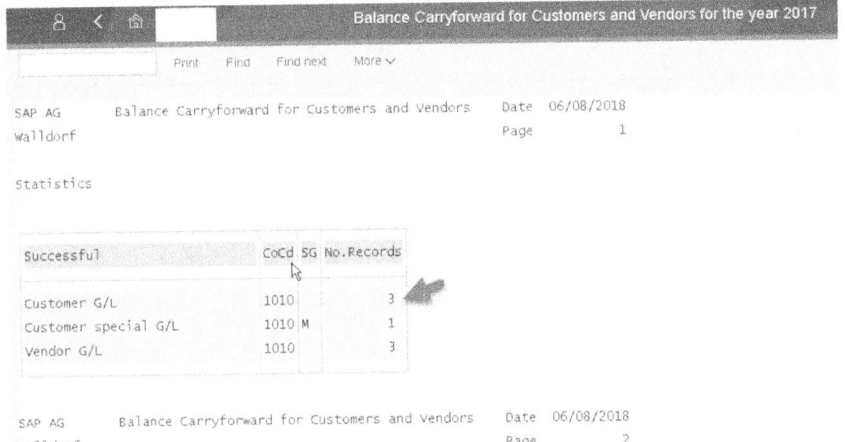

Scroll down the page and Check the customer Balance

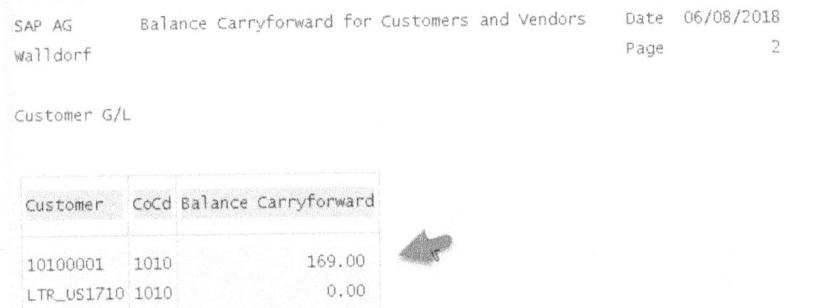

Scroll down the page and Check the vendor Balance

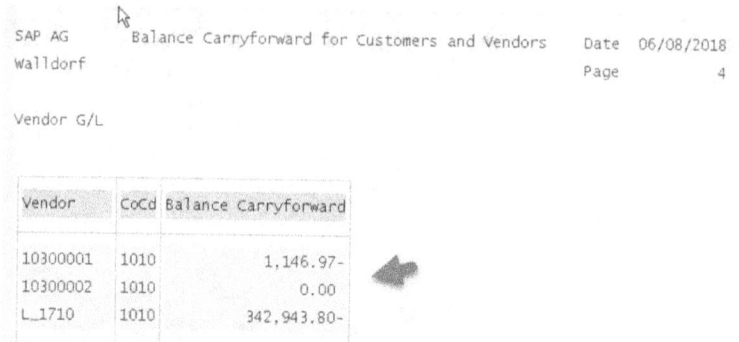

7. Check the Customer Balance for Fiscal year 2018

Double click on Display Customer Balance

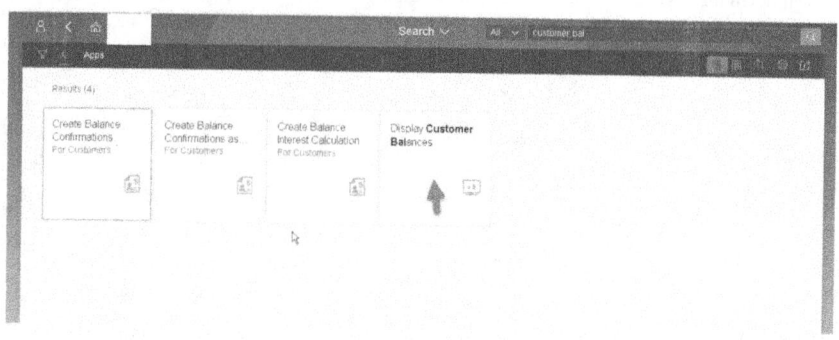

Enter the Company code and Fiscal year'

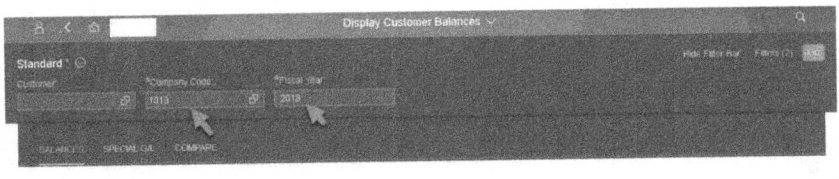

Click on Go button

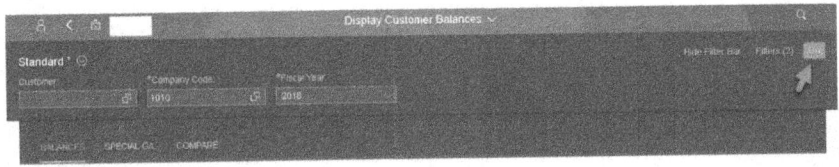

Here we see year 2018 Customer Balance will update

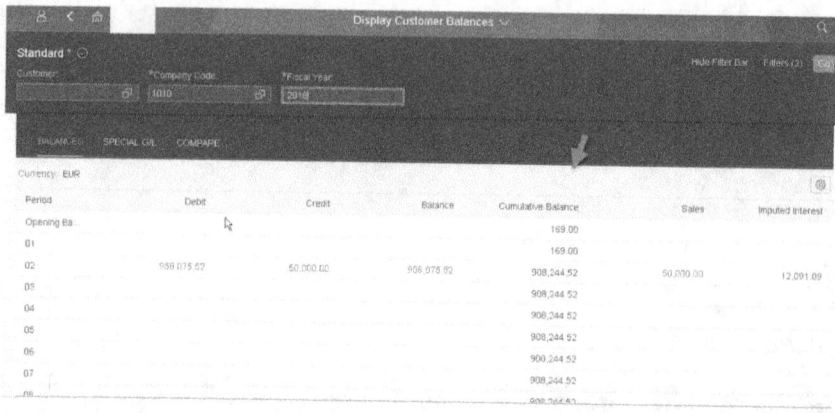

8. Check the Vendor balance for 2018

Double click on Supplier Balances

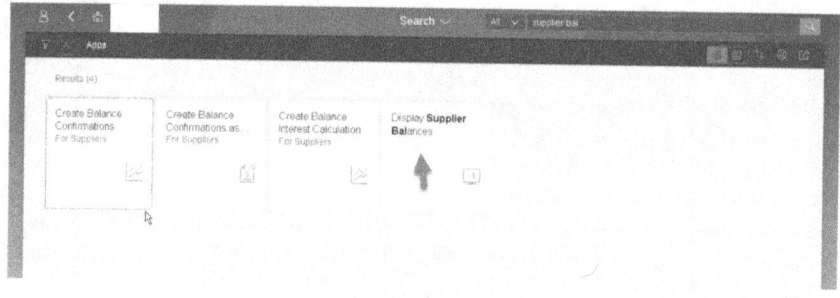

Enter the company code and Fiscal year

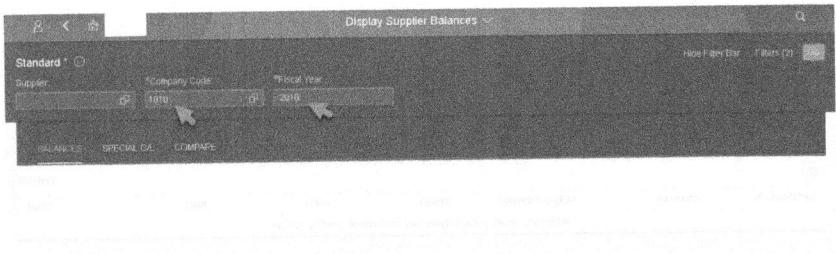

Click on Go Button

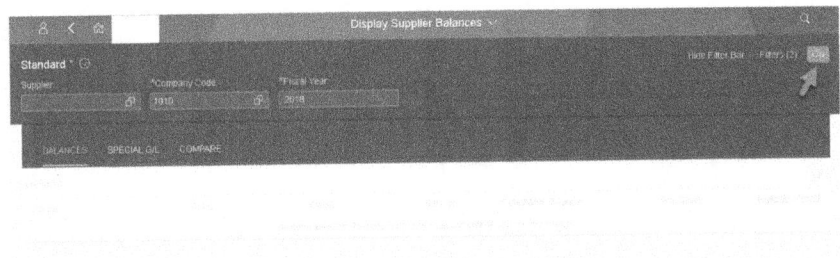

The Balance will update on 2018 fiscal year

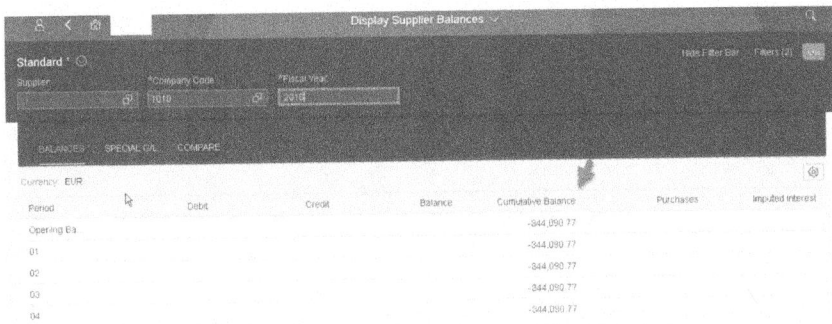

9. Execute Year End Closing

Accounting →Financial Accounting → Fixed Assets → Periodic Processing → Year End Closing →Execute (AJAB)

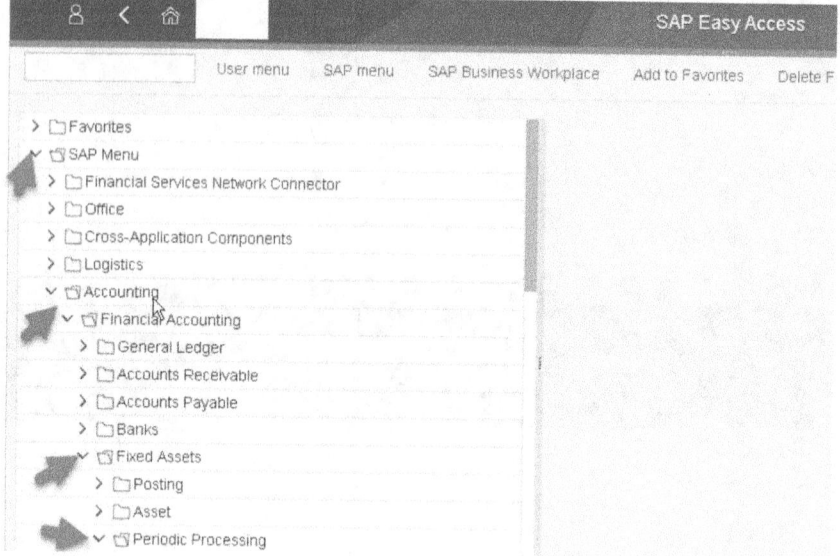

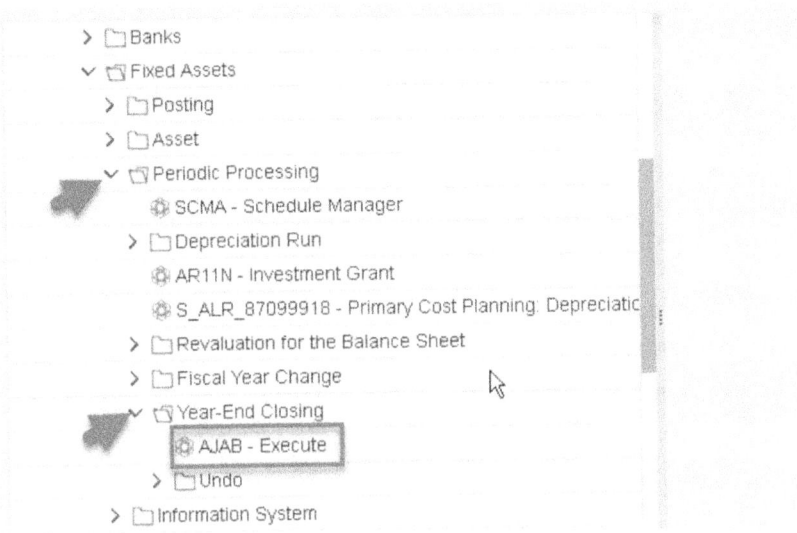

Enter the Company code and Fiscal year to be closed

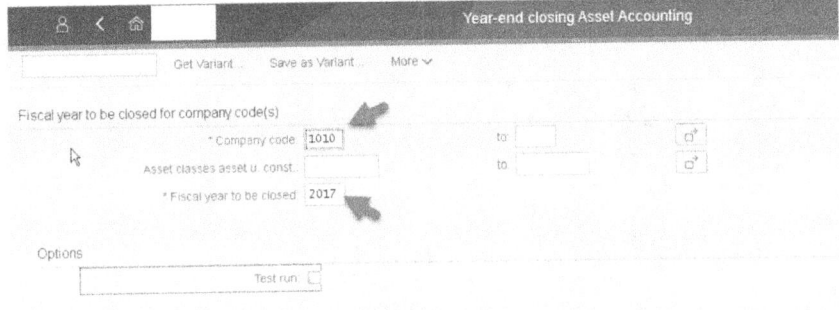

Select the Test Run

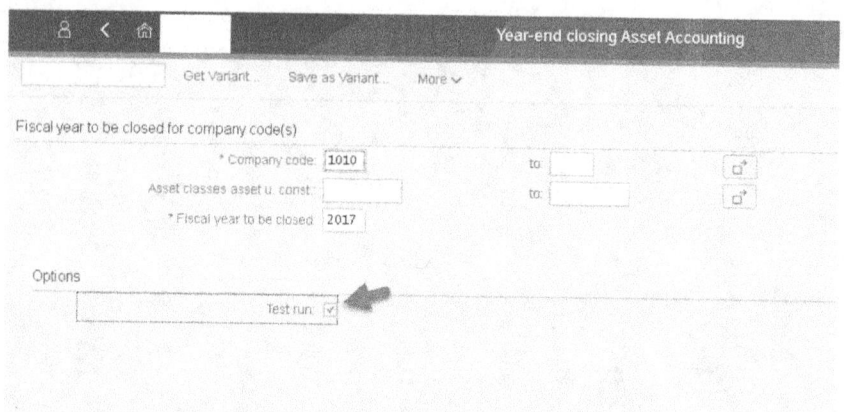

Click on Execute

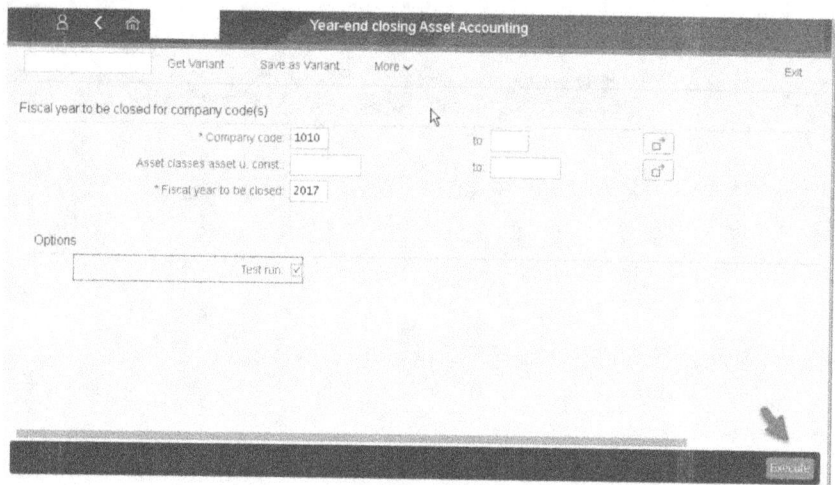

Click to continue for Information Message

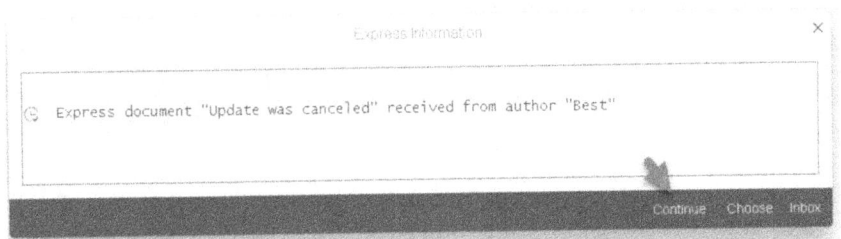

Click to Yes button

Here see No Error

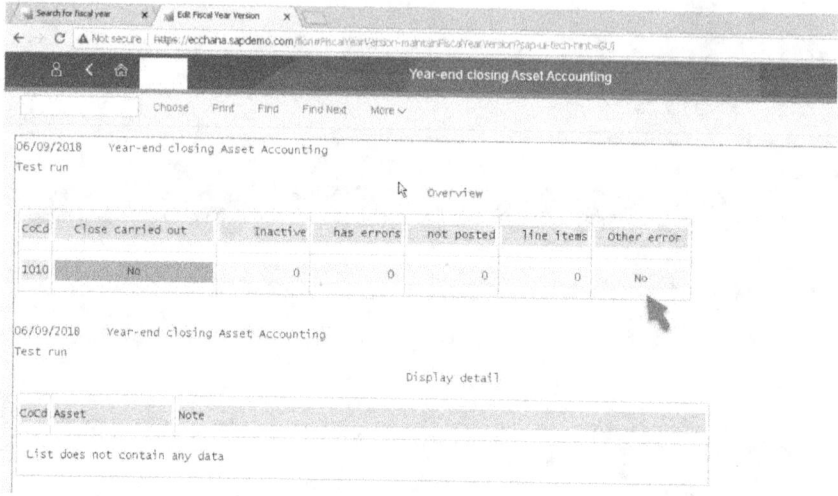

Come to back arrow

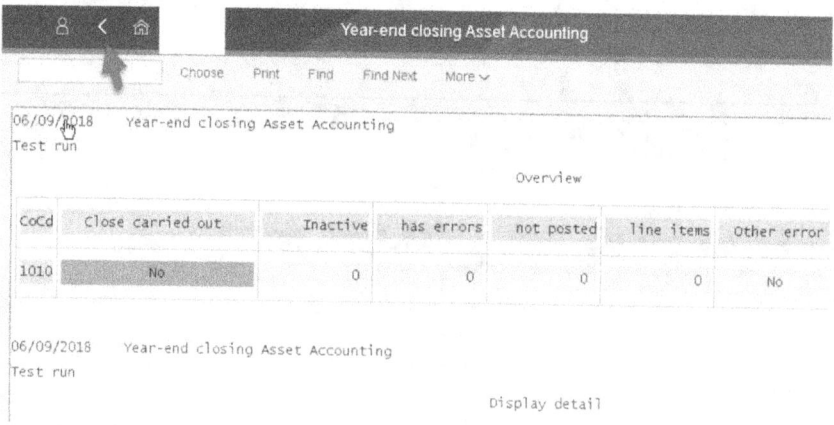

Deselect Test Run

Click on Execute in background Processing

Click on More → Program → Execute in background

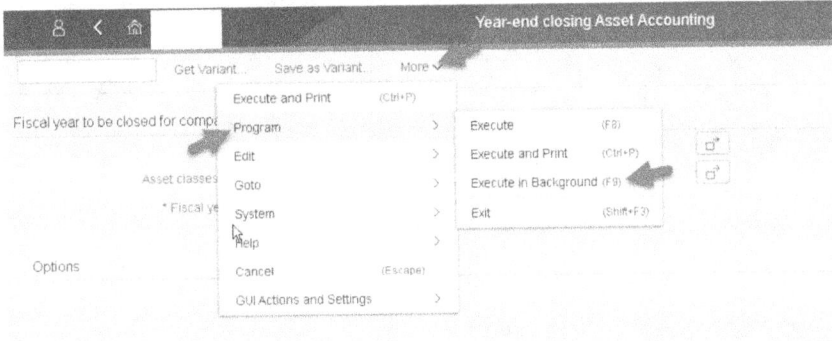

Enter the Output Device is: LP01

Click on continue button

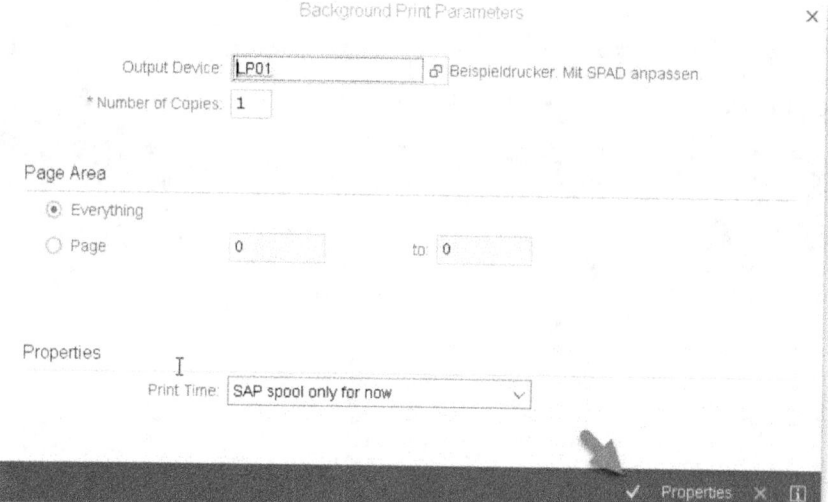

Click on Immediate button

Click on Save button

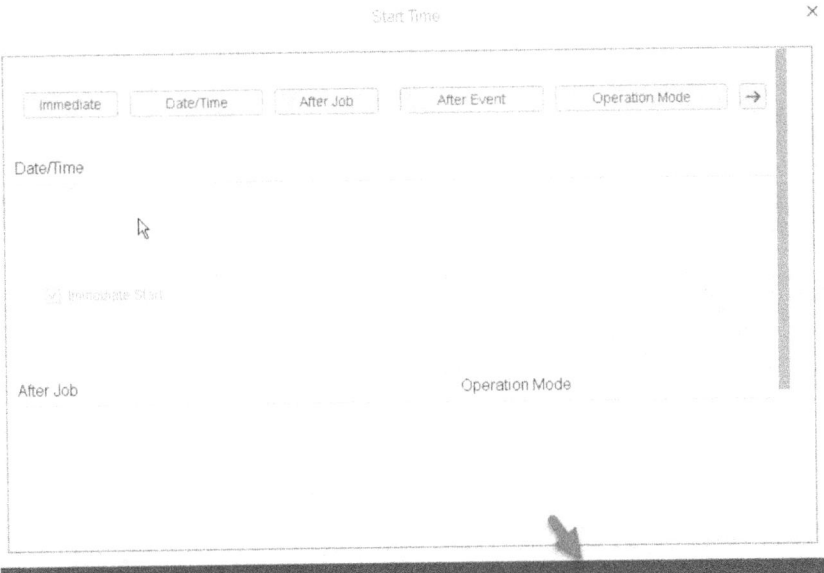

Here we see background job was scheduled for the program RAJABS00

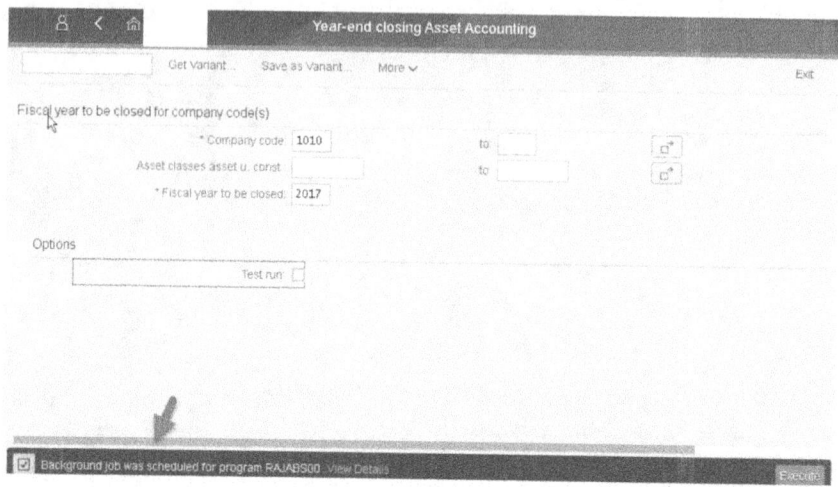

10. View Job Status

Enter the Job Status T-code and click on Enter (sm37)

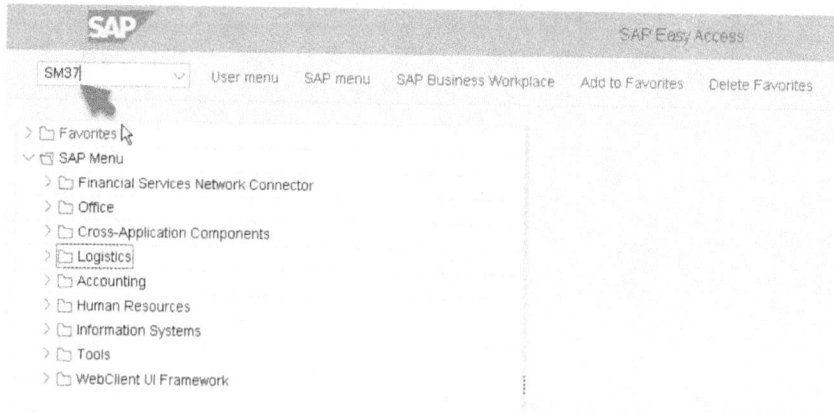

Enter the Job Name

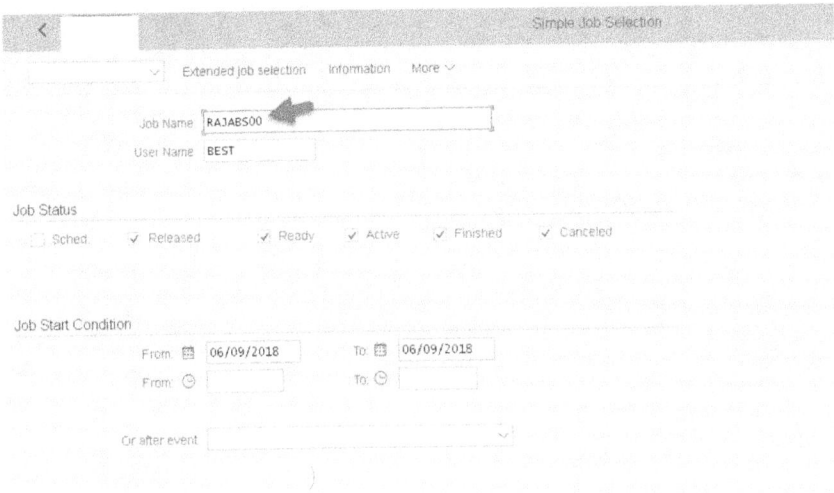

Click on Execute

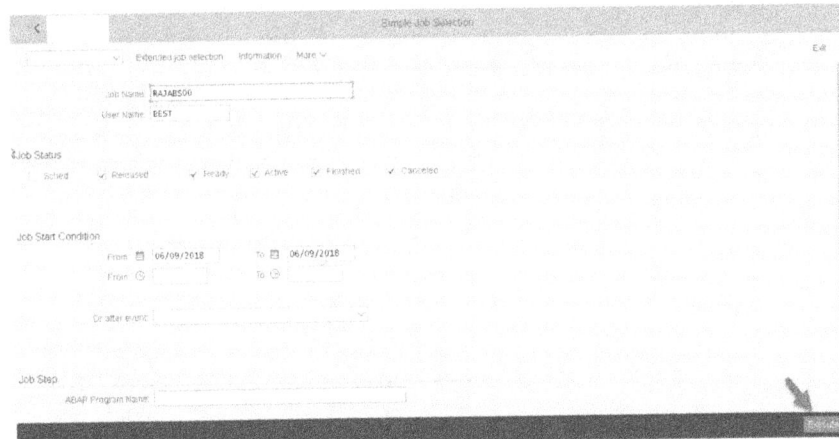

Select the Spool Clock button

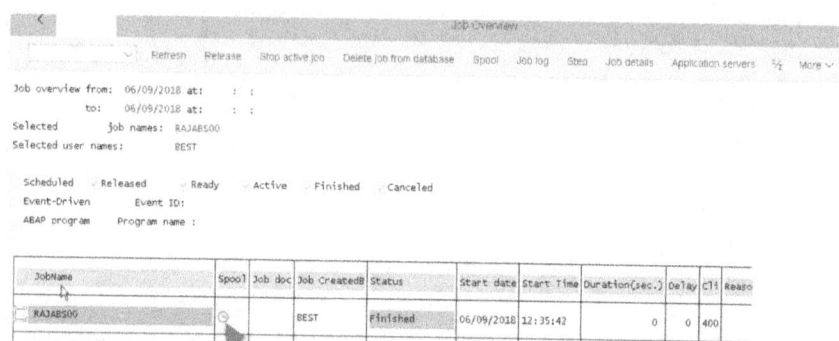

Here we can see Spool Number

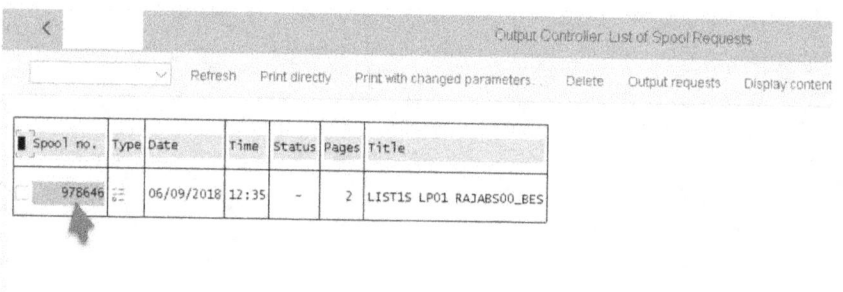

Select the ABAP List button

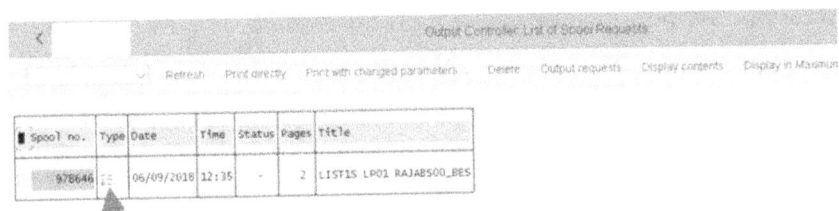

Check the message is Close carried out is yes

Other Error is NO

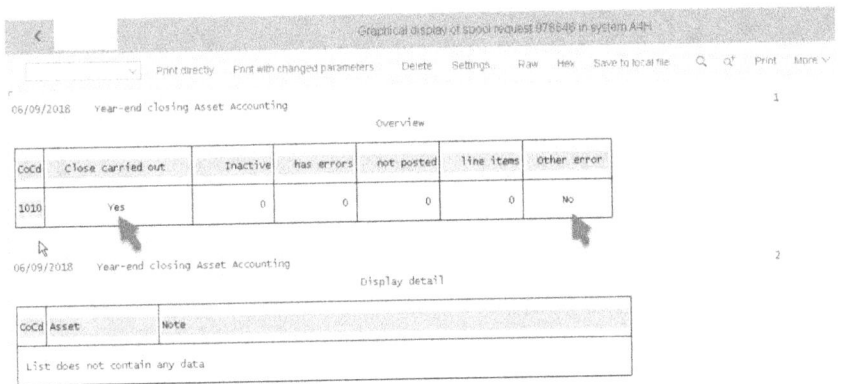

11. Carry forward Gender Ledger Balance to Fiscal year 2018

Accounting →Financial Accounting → Gender Ledger → Periodic Processing → Closing → Carry forward → Balance Carry forward (New)

SAP Easy Access

User menu | SAP menu | SAP Business Workplace | Add to Favorites | Delete Favor

- ∨ 📁 Periodic Processing
  - ⚙ SCMA - Schedule Manager
  - › 📁 Interest Calculation
  - › 📁 Automatic Clearing
  - › 📁 Print Correspondence
  - › 📁 Recurring Entries
  - › 📁 Manual Accruals
  - › 📁 Accruals for Rights Management
  - › 📁 Data Retention Tool
  - › 📁 Data Aging
  - › 📁 Archiving
  - ∨ 📁 Closing
    - › 📁 Check/Count
    - › 📁 Valuate
    - › 📁 Reclassify
    - › 📁 Allocation
    - › 📁 Document
    - › 📁 Report
    - ∨ 📁 Carrying Forward
      - ⚙ FAGLGVTR - Balance Carryforward (New)
      - ⚙ IPMCARRYFORWARD - Revenue Recognition for

Enter the Ledger, company code and carry forward to fiscal year

Select the check box for Test Run and Results List

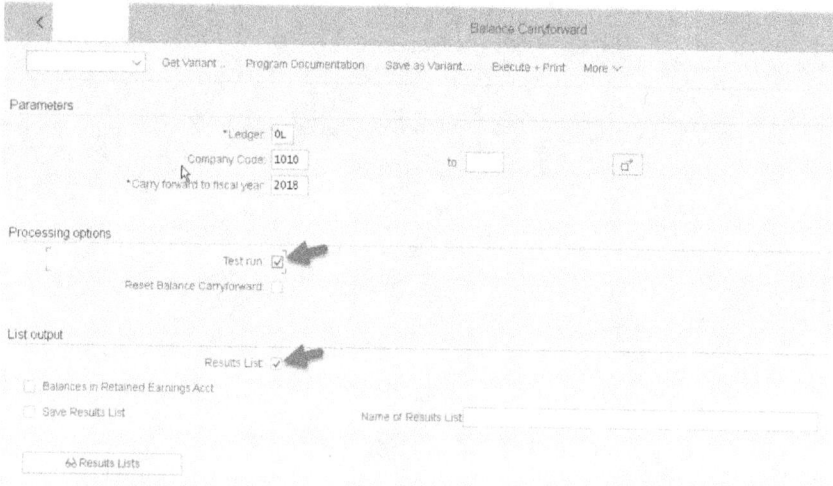

Click on Execute

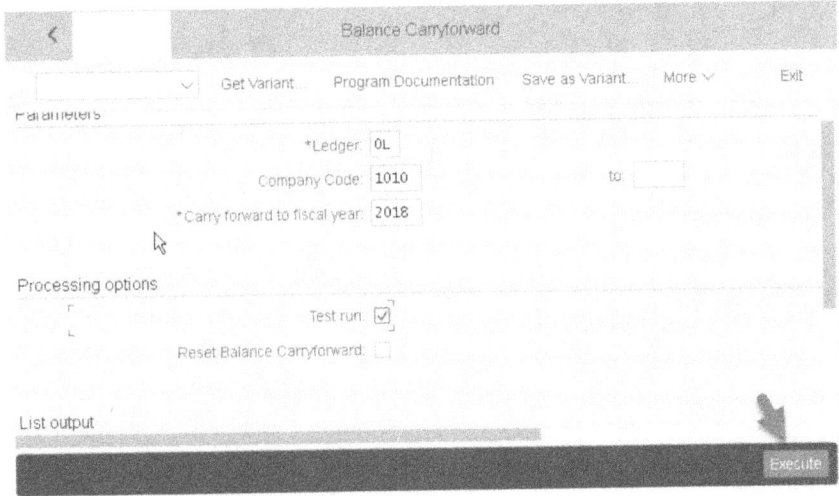

Here see All balance carry forward fiscal year 2018

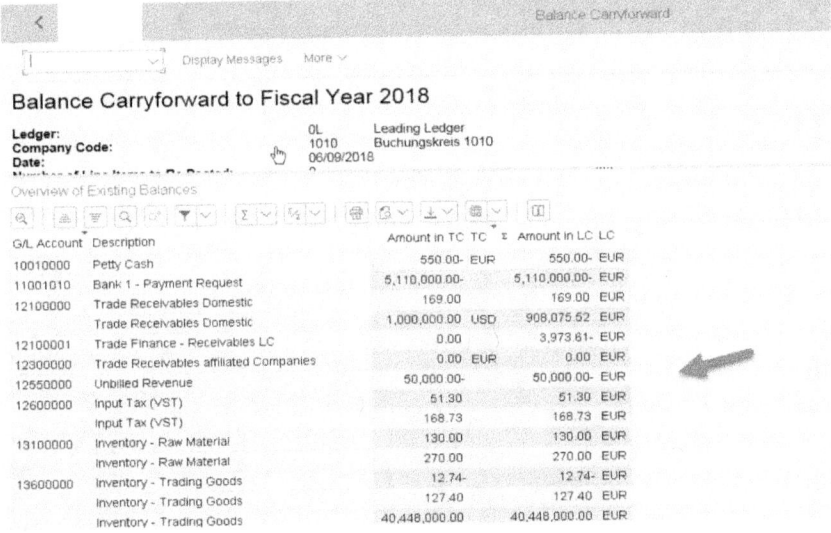

Come to back arrow

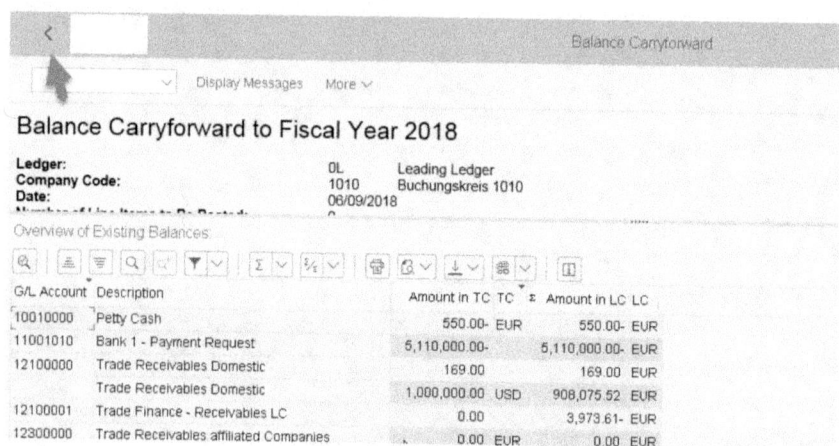

Deselect the Test Run

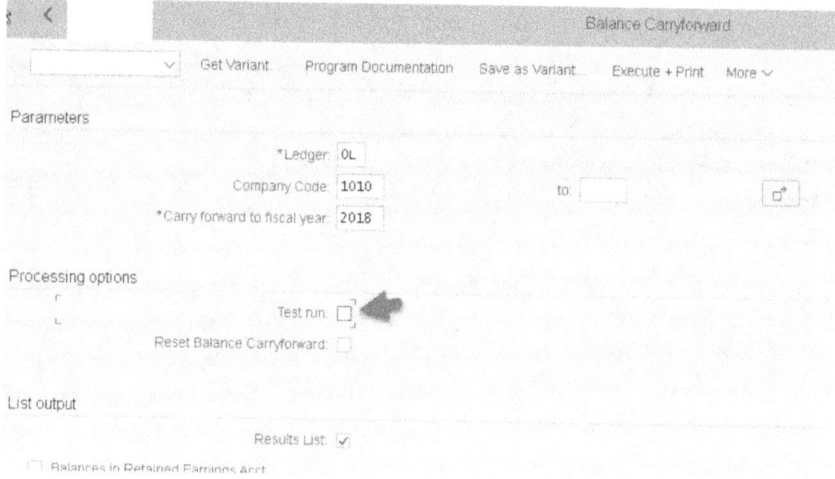

Click to Execute

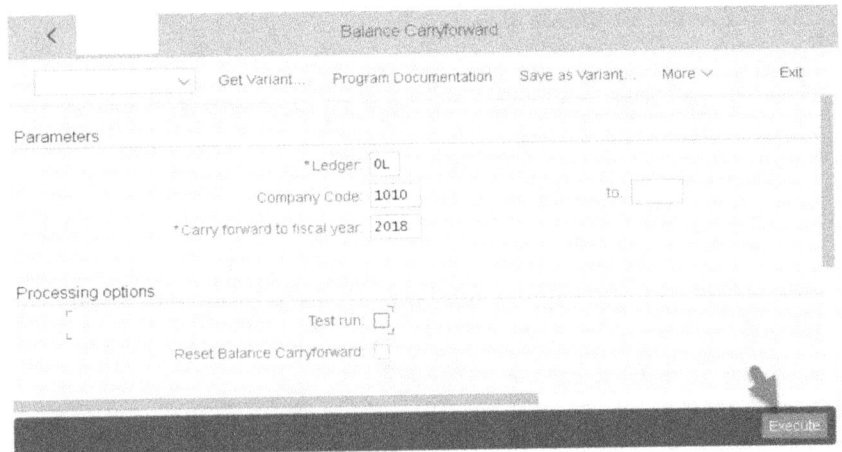

All Gender ledger balance successfully carry forward

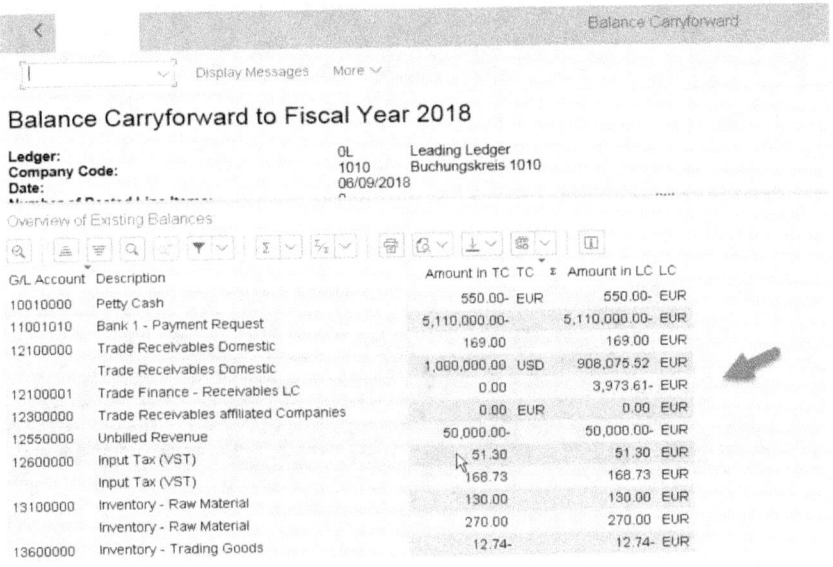

12. Checking Gender ledger Balance for Fiscal year 2018

Double click on Display G/L Account Balances

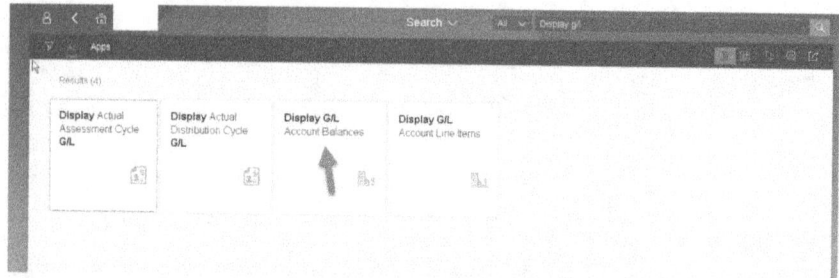

Enter the company code and Enter New fiscal year for 2018

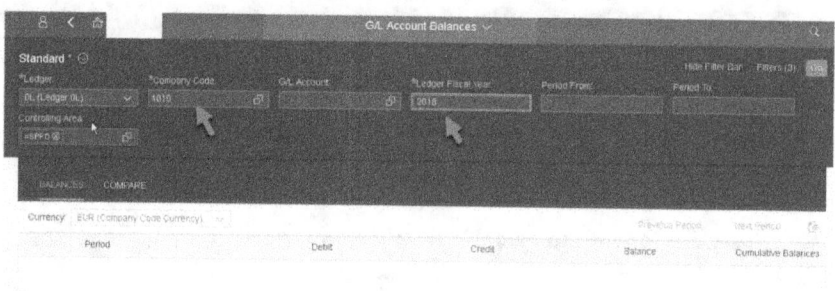

Click as Go

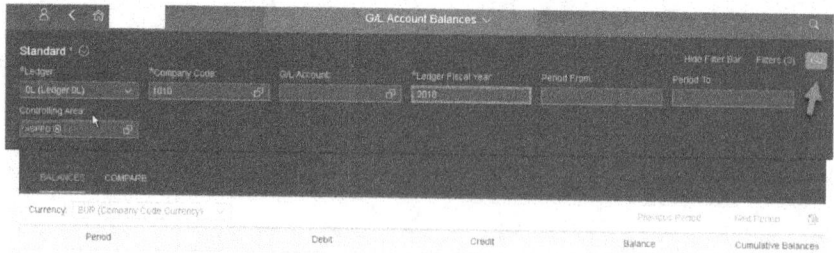

Here see All Gender Ledger Balance Carry Forward to fiscal year 2018

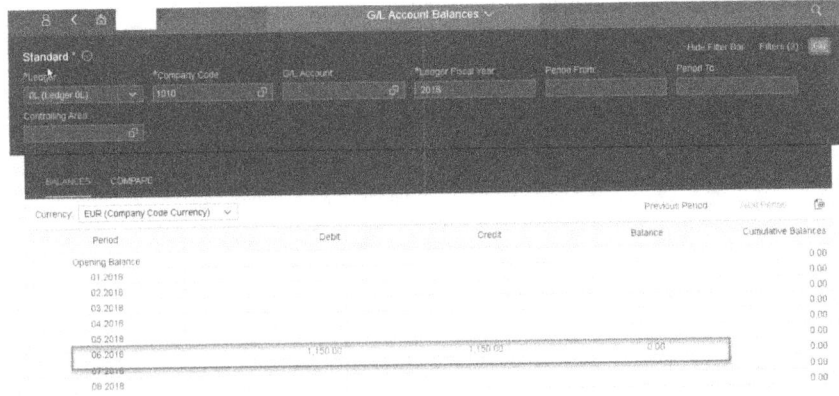

13. Change to New Fiscal Year for 2018

Enter the T-code as: AJRW

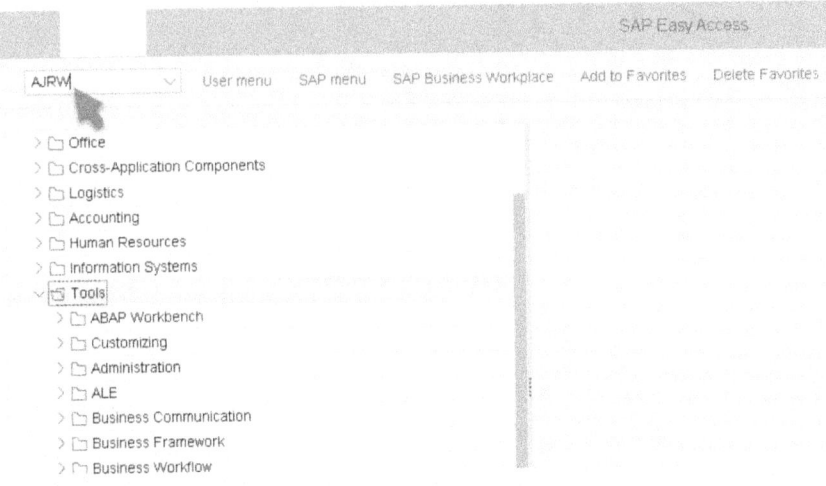

Enter the Company code and New Fiscal year

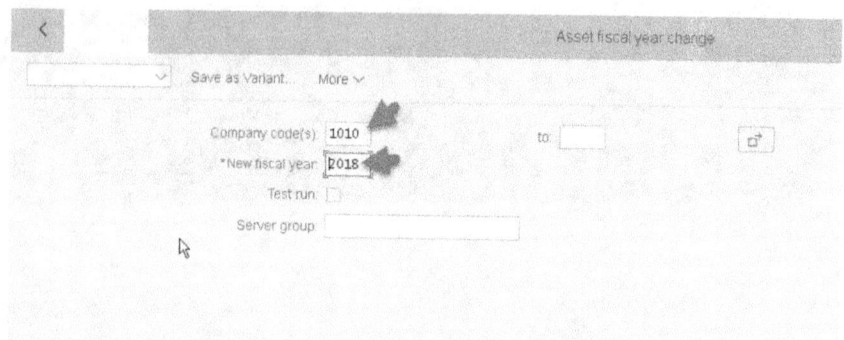

Select check box for Test Run

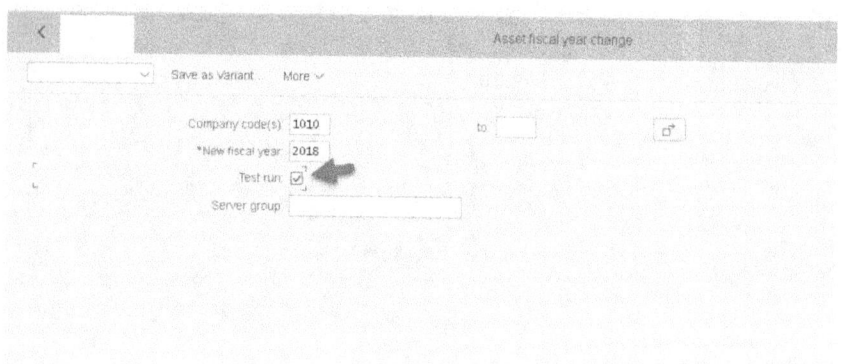

Click to Execute

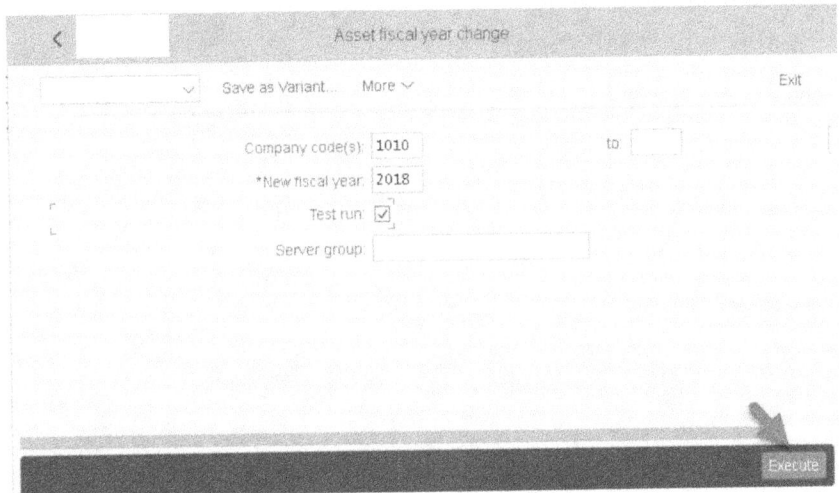

Click to yes button

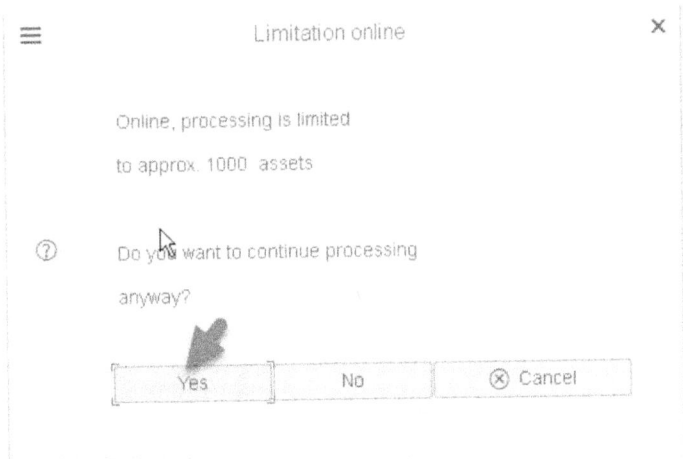

Here see status is Green No Error

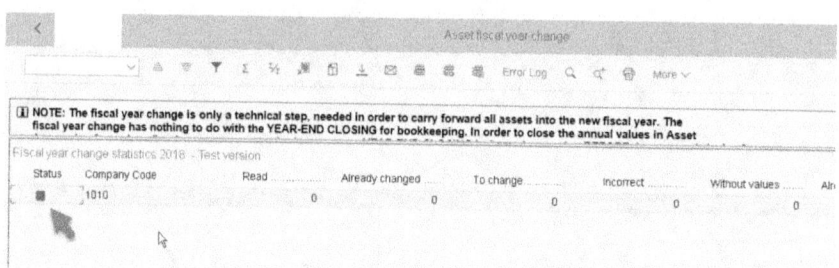

Come to back arrow

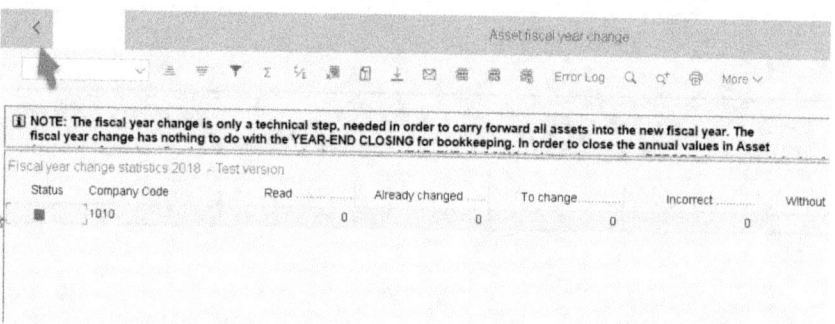

Deselect Test Run

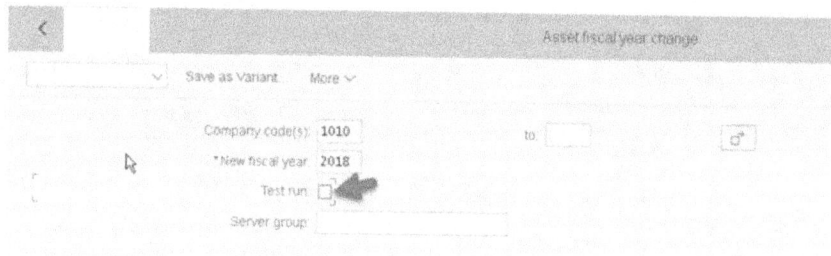

Click to Execute in background

More menu → Program → Execute in background

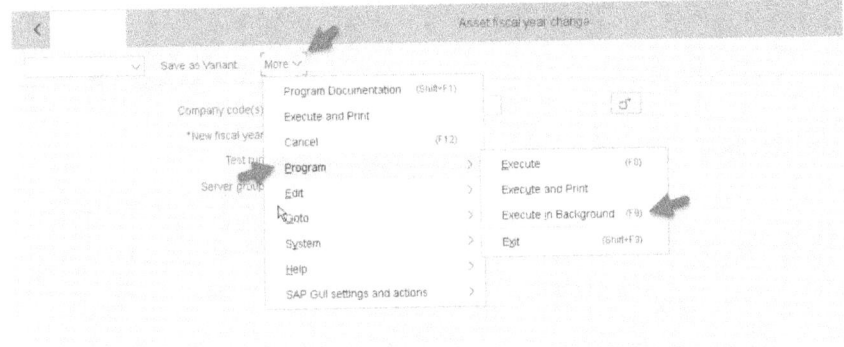

Enter the Output Device as: LP01

Click on Continue button

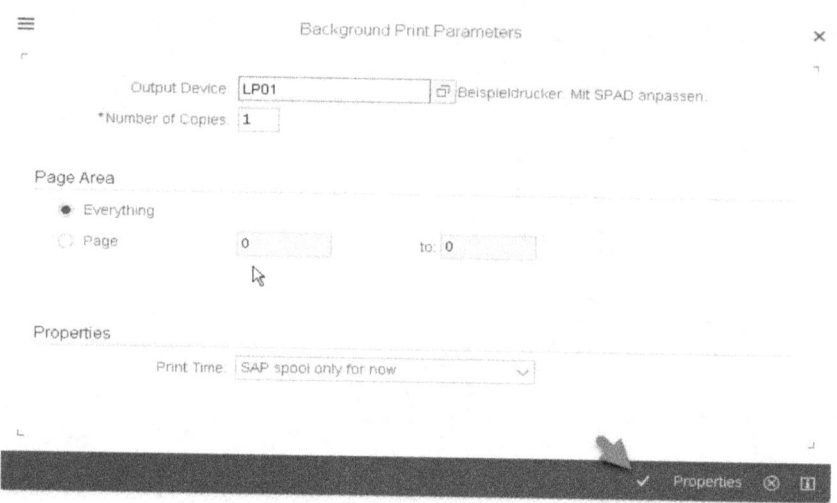

Click on

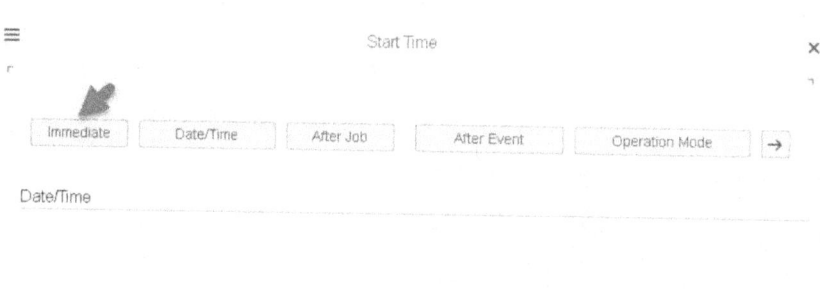

Date/Time

After Job   Operation Mode

Click to Save

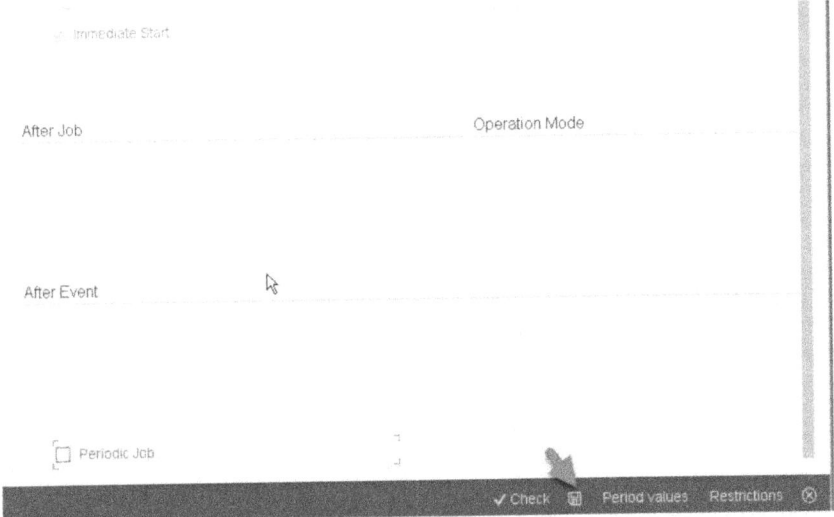

Here we see background job was scheduled for program as: RAJAWE00

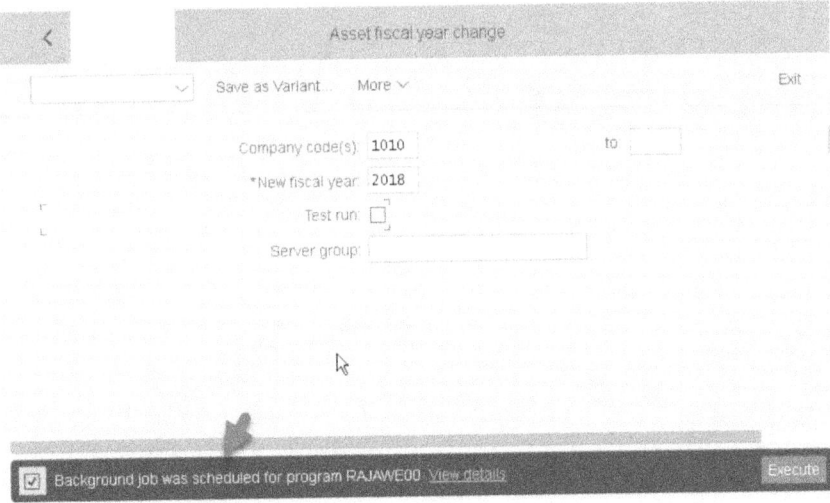

14. View Job Status

Enter the Job Status T-code and click on Enter

				SAP Easy Access	
SM37	User menu	SAP menu	SAP Business Workplace	Add to Favorites	Delete Favorites

> 🗁 Favorites
∨ 🗁 SAP Menu
  > 🗁 Financial Services Network Connector
  > 🗁 Office
  > 🗁 Cross-Application Components
  > 🗁 Logistics
  > 🗁 Accounting
  > 🗁 Human Resources
  > 🗁 Information Systems
  > 🗁 Tools
  > 🗁 WebClient UI Framework

Enter the Job Name as: RAJAWE00

Simple Job Selection

Extended job selection   Information   More ∨

Job Name: RAJAWE00
User Name: BEST

Job Status

☐ Sched   ☑ Released   ☑ Ready   ☑ Active   ☑ Finished   ☑ Canceled

Job Start Condition

From: 📅 06/09/2018   To: 📅 06/09/2018
From: 🕒   To: 🕒

Or after event:

Click on Execute

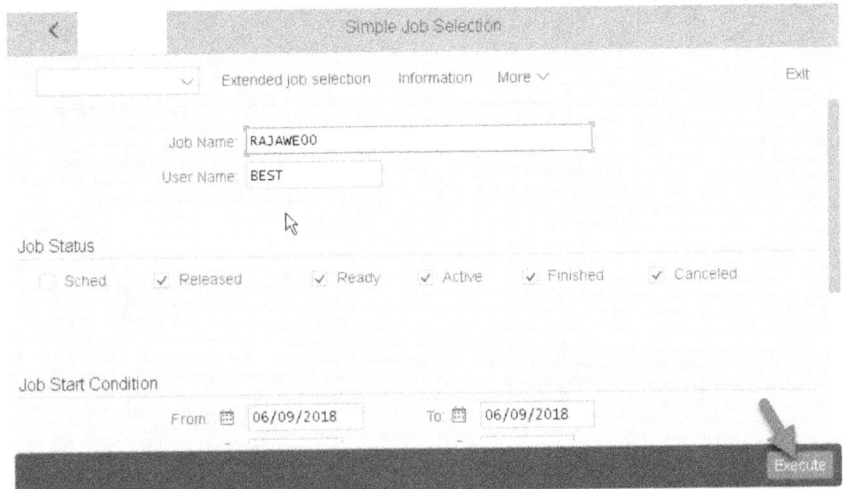

Select the Spool Clock button

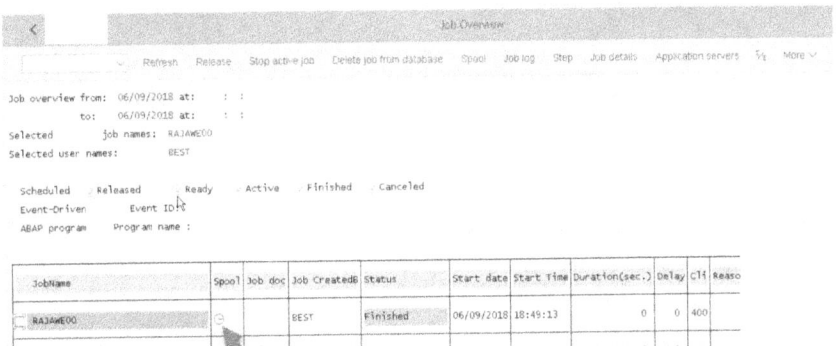

Here see Spool Number

Spool no.	Type	Date	Time	Status	Pages	Title
978647		06/09/2018	18:49	-	2	LIST1S LP01 RAJAWE00_BES

Select the ABAP List button

Spool no.	Type	Date	Time	Status	Pages	Title
978647		06/09/2018	18:49	-	2	LIST1S LP01 RAJAWE00_BES

Check the message is Status is Green

nothing to do with the YEAR-END CLOSING for bookkeeping. In order to close the annual values in Asset Accounting for a given fiscal year, you are required to carry out YEAR-END CLOSING in Asset Accounting BEFORE the year-end closing for the general ledger.

Fiscal year change statistics 2018

Status	Company Code	Read	Already ch	Changed ..	Incorrect	Without va	Alrea
■	1010	0	0	0	0	0	

Type	Message text
■	1010: Recalculation of depreciation started (see log -> ARMO)

15. Display Closed Fiscal year check for 2017

Accounting → Financial Accounting → Fixed Assets → Periodic Processing → Year End Closing → Year End Closing → Undo → Entire company code

```
SAP Easy Access

                            User menu   SAP menu   SAP Business Workplace   Add to Favorites   Delete Favorites

> Favorites
∨ SAP Menu
  > Financial Services Network Connector
  > Office
  > Cross-Application Components
  > Logistics
  ∨ Accounting
    ∨ Financial Accounting
      > General Ledger
      > Accounts Receivable
      > Accounts Payable
      > Banks
      ∨ Fixed Assets
        > Posting
        > Asset
        ∨ Periodic Processing
```

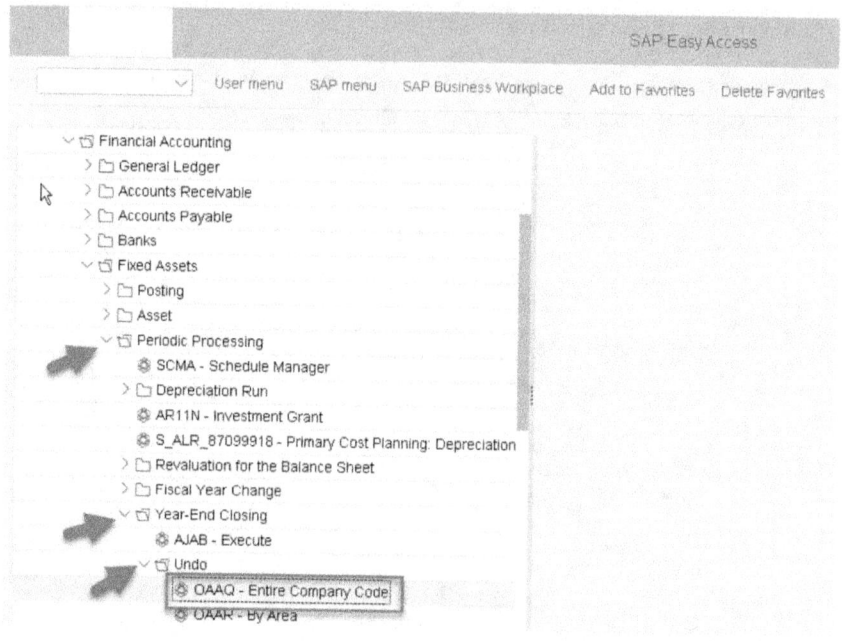

Here see company code fiscal year closed in 2017

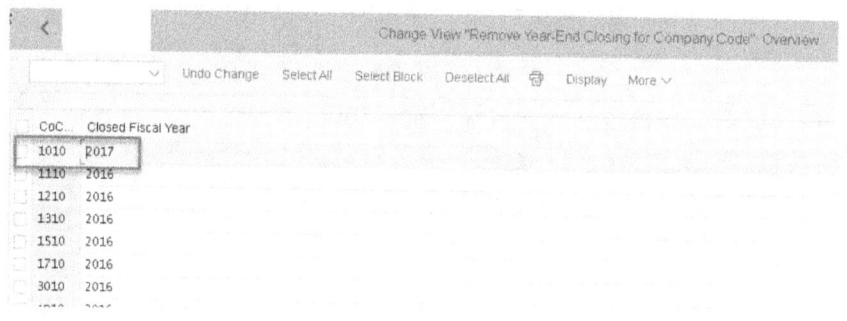

www.ingramcontent.com/pod-product-compliance
Lightning Source LLC
Chambersburg PA
CBHW072054230526
45479CB00010B/1002